Seven Rules for Hiring *Extraordinary Talent*

A Business Story by

Richard J. Pinsker, CMC, FIMC

Published by: HRD Press, Inc.
                  22 Amherst Road
                  Amherst, MA 01002
                  1-800-822-2801
                  413-253-3488
                  413-253-3490 (fax)
                  www.hrdpress.com

ISBN 978-1-59996-175-0

Editorial Services: Robert W. Carkhuff
Production Services: Jean S. Miller
Cover Design: Eileen Klockars

In memory of
James O'Rourke

Humorist and great friend.

"We miss you"

Thanks!

Two good friends and authors provided sound advice to the creation of this book. Jim Carey developed the idea for this business style book with me back in 1994, and provided great editorial commentary for this edition. Vic Prushan, who has a cutting style of humor and writing, gave excellent input for dialogue creation and character development.

Thanks to the many clients who unknowingly have provided the seven rules for hiring extraordinary talent.

Seven Rules for Hiring Extraordinary Talent

Content

Introduction

"Have you ever hired someone whom you should never have hired in the first place?" If you answered "yes," then you're not alone.

Few hiring managers have ever been taught how to hire successfully. That's unfortunate! Left to chance, hiring is a decision that could have a major impact on a company's most important asset—its employees.

There is nothing magic about making a good hiring decision. It's a skill that anyone can learn and apply. The *Seven Rules for Hiring Extraordinary Talent* will serve as a guide for anyone involved in the hiring process. Ignoring these rules can be expensive.

For example, an experienced salesperson is hired but the person lasts only three months. What are some of the costs of losing that person?

1. Lost potential revenue from sales that did not materialize.

2. More lost revenue from sales while you seek a replacement.

3. Customer reaction to lack of continuity of sales representation.

4. Time recruiting and interviewing new candidates.

5. Replacement expenses, such as recruitment fees, travel, etc.

6. Training time for the new sales person.

During the past thirty years working with companies to find, select and hire key employees, I have observed and noted the most common mistakes that have prevented managers from getting the best hiring results. Adhering to the *Seven Rules* ensures that these mistakes will not be made!

None of the rules are profound. All of them can be implemented rather easily, and, in doing so, will result in more objective and predictable hiring decisions. You will hire people who get the results you want.

Some readers may find the ideas presented in this book provide a logical framework to what they are already doing. Others will find new ideas to add to their hiring skills. Hopefully most readers will be stimulated and encouraged to think outside of their recruitment/hiring system box and try a new approach to hire the best people.

This is a business book told in a story format. The story is light-hearted; the subject matter is serious.

Chapters one through seven treat each of the rules separately. Chapter eight summarizes the rules and provides an action plan to implement them.

The story relates a typical Thursday coffee get together between old friends. The characters are composites of personal friends and their contributions are based on actual employment situations.

The characters:

Pat (The Pupil and Narrator of the Story), is in his mid-thirties and is President and one of the founders of a company that is beginning to grow and prosper. Company sales are about $10 million.

Roger (The Retiree), is in his mid-fifties and is retired. He founded a company that grew to over $250 million and sold it a few years ago.

Charles (The Consultant), is in his early sixties and is a management consultant who specializes in executive selection. He has known Roger for over twenty years and has helped him build his management team.

Harry (The Heckler), is in his late-thirties and is Vice President of Sales for a small, stable $8 million company.

Join these friends as they discover how to hire extraordinary talent.

Dick Pinsker

Chapter One

Hire to Specific Performance Expectations

"A non-fat latte with no foam."

The Perfect Blend coffee shop in Roseville is usually pretty empty at 6:30 in the morning. Traffic begins to pick up after 7:00—business people on their way to work, a couple stopping by after their morning walk, and others just stopping in to use the free Internet service. With inside and outside patio seating, there's always room for a small, casual or confidential meeting.

This has become a monthly ritual—the four of us meeting for coffee on the third Thursday of each month. Our personal friendship has made this a monthly commitment. It's quite unusual when one of us misses this rendezvous.

Charles was the first to arrive after me. Charles is in his mid 60's, tan, keeps in reasonable shape and always is on time. In fact, he is quite compulsive in showing up before the appointed hour of 7:00 a.m. Today was no exception. We often kid him about his obsession with being early.

Roger was next to arrive. At fifty-five, he had taken his electronics company public just before the 2000 stock market downturn. He's a smart businessman who knew how to bring out the best in his employees. He was very demanding of his employees and has high expectations for himself. That was the way it was in his company. His competitive nature served him well in business.

Charles is a management consultant who had worked with Roger while he was building his company. What started out as a consultant-client relationship turned into a twenty-year friendship. Charles worked with Roger and his management team in developing an executive recruitment and selection process. I need to talk to both of them about my hiring problems. If I don't solve my personnel problems quickly, my board of directors will make me the number one hiring problem.

Harry arrived a few minutes after 7:00. He quickly ordered his espresso—three shots, and then joined us on the patio. A Vice President of Sales for a software company, Harry spends more time on the golf course then most people I know. How he does it is his secret.

Not only do we meet once a month for coffee, but we try to arrange a golf foursome a number of times a years. It's more social than competitive golf, although Harry takes his game fairly seriously. The round of golf is like an extension of our monthly coffee gatherings. We play, talk about whatever comes to mind and just enjoy ourselves.

Although a few of us have known each other for over a decade, the four of us have been meeting for coffee for over a year We feel pretty much at ease with one another. We usually keep our conversation light—kind of a catch-up on what's going on in each others' lives. If one of us actually has a serious issue, the others listen and offer suggestions or opinions. I guess this was my day.

"Guys, I need some advice," I popped in after one of Harry's raunchier stories. "I have a serious hiring problem. I know you all have heard this before. My hiring track record never seems to improve. I need to hire several significant management types in the next six months. One of the three needs to be hired quickly or I may be the next requirement effort for my company."

"This sounds serious," said Roger "What's the problem? Who are you unhappy with this time?"

"You remember me bragging about the new Sales VP I hired six month ago? Well, it's not working out. I could give you a lot of reasons, but the bottom line is he hasn't moved us forward with any major accounts. My board of directors is on my backside for not having addressed this situation sooner. I need to replace him quickly."

Selling has never been my strength. After receiving my mechanical engineering degree from Wisconsin, I worked in product development for one of the largest switching device manufacturers in Milwaukee. Within three years I was promoted to manage a large product development group. Shortly thereafter, a recruiter contacted me to come to Sacramento to become the vice president of engineering for a start-up company. A few years later, because of differences with the president regarding product direction, I left with several others to form our current company. We've found our market niche, and now we need to take advantage of it. At 32, I could become a dethroned president if I don't solve this recruitment problem quickly.

"Pat," Charles said, "we've had some of this discussion before, when you were interviewing candidates the first time you were recruiting that

Sales VP. But you never wanted to take the time to review your hiring process."

"I know. I know. There never seems to be enough hours in a day to do everything."

"You know I'm a firm believer that employees are a company's most important asset. Roger says 'cash is king.' I would agree it is important. However, without a strong management team, cash would be hard to obtain and manage. I guess it's the old-cart-before-the-horse syndrome."

Our company spent three years in product development and has just recently begun to take off. I'm expected to lead the effort. Spending 12 to 14 hour days working haven't been enough to cover all the bases. I know hiring is important, but so is product development, financing, operations and everything else.

"I know that's your field of expertise," I responded to Charles. "Roger had also recommended we get together. You helped him build his management team way back when his company was our size."

"Pat, we made a bunch of poor hiring decisions in our early days," said Roger. "Charles did coach our management on how to do a better job in hiring people, especially executives. In fact, Charles recently presented a talk to the Silicon Valley Management Association in Palo Alto on the subject of making better hiring decisions."

"Actually, the title was 'Seven Rules for Hiring Extraordinary Talent,'" interrupted Charles. "Audiences seem to remember items when they're numbered."

"I'm sorry I missed it. I would have driven down to the Bay Area to hear you. How can I play 'catch-up' so I don't blow it again? I've got a lot at stake! My job is on the line."

"Okay. If you guys can put up with the discussion, and maybe even Harry contributes, I'll take care of the tab this morning."

"Big deal," said Harry sarcastically. "For a lousy 20 bucks he gets all our great advice," he added jokingly.

"OK. I'll tell you what I'll do. If we spend this morning on helping me get some answers, I'll pick up lunch and libations at golf next month."

"Now we're talking the right deal," Harry added.

* * *

After the waitress served our orders—bagel and cream cheese for Charles and my self, a blueberry muffin for Roger, and a scrambled-egg and bacon-plate for Harry—Charles said, "As we all are golfers, perhaps I can relate some of the Seven Rules to golf."

"That's sounds like an interesting way to get started," I responded.

"The first thing we do when we arrive at a golf course is hit some balls on the driving range to warm up," said Harry. "Can you tie that in with one of your rules," he asked Charles?

"Thanks for the perfect lead," responded Charles. "When you get to the driving range you select a club and target. Without having a specific target in mind, you'll never hit it. That's the way the mind and body work in golf."

"Wasn't it Harvey Penick who used the phrase, 'Take Dead Aim'?" asked Roger.

"That's an analogy to my first rule," said Charles. "I call it '**Hire to Specific Performance Expectations**'. This first rule is the most important one. It boils down to knowing precisely why you want to hire someone in the first place."

"I usually use a job description to define my hiring requirements," I chimed in. "Anything wrong with that?"

"Many companies use job descriptions to define their hiring requirements. Unfortunately, job descriptions list duties and responsibilities, activities in which to indulge. I have found a more useful approach to defining a hiring requirement. It begins with identifying the results you expect the new hire to achieve during the first year. In that way, you're focusing on achieving results, or performance, rather than just the duties or activities of a job.

"Once you've identified those results, then it is much easier to develop a list of hiring criteria— experiences and skills a person has achieved in the past that best parallel what you expect them to accomplish in your company. Remember, the best predictor of future performance is past performance."

"Hey, Pat," said Charles, "Let me give you an example of what I am talking about. Picture both of us on the fringe of a green, with the hole about 15 feet up and over a slight rise. The result we want to achieve is to hit the ball so that it drops in the cup, or comes as close as we can get it to the cup. That should be the only thought in our mind. Neither of us cares how the other will do it. In other words, we don't care whether we use a chip shot or a putt, just that we get it to the cup.

"What we bring is successful experience doing similar shots in the past. Your previous experience with shots like that may suggest you use a wedge rather than a putter to get the ball close to the cup. My experience with these fringe shots is to use a putter. Neither choice is right or wrong, but depends on our previous successes with that kind of shot.

"Similarly, if you identify the specific results you want a new hire to achieve, you can determine the experience and skills a candidate should have to accomplish those results. It's the results that drive the action, not just the action alone."

"I see," I said. "If I want a salesperson to book a million dollars worth of new business in the first year, then I want to consider candidates who have been successful in booking a million dollars worth of business in a similar environment. I need to focus on the results I want this salesperson to achieve. I shouldn't be concerned how he accomplished it, assuming it was within our company's values. That's just another way of saying past performance is the best predictor of future performance."

"Now you've got it!" said Charles.

"Here's another example of what Charles is saying," said Roger, overhearing the conversation. "We were looking for a manufacturing manager for one of our high volume, precision production operations. One of the performance expectations for this manufacturing manager was to improve the yield of our production by at least 5% per year. The candidate that caught our attention was from a similar production operation where he had increased the yield by over 18% in three years."

"Did you hire him?" I asked.

"We sure did. But that was after all the other steps in the hiring process, including references, verified that he had the right experience and fit with our management style.

"Pat, there's another reason for identifying the specific results you want a new hire to achieve. When one of my employees said he wanted to hire someone, we asked him to justify the need by making a list of the results he expected this person to achieve. That showed me he had a very clear picture of what he wanted to accomplish by the hire. It justified the cost of the hire."

"I understand this coming up with a list of expected goals or results, but should I look for someone who has achieved those specific results previously, perhaps for another company?" I asked.

"That would be ideal," Charles responded, "but you seldom have that luxury. Instead, you need to determine the critical experiences and skills a candidate should have to achieve those results. In your example of a salesperson, perhaps it's the knowledge of your customer or market, or perhaps an understanding of your products."

"Yes, those are important candidate requirements based on my list of expected results," I added.

"And that's only part of it. Skills and experience play a major role in deciding which candidates should be considered. However, you mentioned achieving results within your company values.

You're right! It is important to ensure that there is a cultural fit between the candidate and your company."

"I assume you mean by 'cultural fit' the way we go about our business, from an ethical standard."

"That's all part of it," Charles responded. "Every company takes on a personality as it develops and grows. Their personality reflects the beliefs and style of company management.

"For example, some companies expect their employees to work long hours. Perhaps they hire fewer employees, expecting each to contribute well beyond the capacity of one person. Or they believe working long hours demonstrates employee loyalty and dedication to the company. If this is their management style, you better be prepared to share those long hours."

"As another example, Roger's company stressed a 'hands-on' management style. Managers were expected to be out and about—with customers, manufacturing people, and others to insure they knew what was going on. The last thing Roger wanted was a manager who spent the day at his or her desk. And Roger clearly set the example," said Charles.

"Of course someone has to fit in with our management style, and share our beliefs," I commented, "But there must be a number of characteristics that a candidate should have to be successful in our environment. How do I get everyone in our company to identify and understand which characteristics will ensure a candidate will be successful?" I asked.

"Roger, tell Pat how you determined candidate characteristics for a successful fit in your company," suggested Charles.

"Company culture and values are set by the founders, owners or top management of corporations. It's part of the way they conduct themselves and their business," he answered. "You notice it in management's behavior. You see it in managements' decision-making process. You live with it in the type of people hired."

"Yes, I understand."

Roger continued. "Company culture and management style should be identified in writing, so that different levels of management and supervision recognize it in a candidate during the hiring process. That's what we did at our company fairly early on in our history."

"How did you do that?"

"We did it during a management retreat. It was our Vice President of Human Resources' idea. She felt we were missing something during our interviews with management candidates; something we overlooked. And she was right. We had been concentrating on experience and skills fit, and not consciously thinking about cultural fit. It showed up at it's worse in the management style of a few of the executives we hired. We had trouble holding onto good employees.

"She ran a session in which we came up with a list of the behavior patterns that reflected the management style of our best executives," he continued. "As an example, one was 'the ability to handle stress well'. You may not know from seeing me on

10

the golf course, but I'm not an easy guy to work for; very demanding. Some might say unrealistically demanding. But it's nothing personal with the employee. My management team understood this. It was part of our company culture. People who couldn't manage stress weren't successful on our team," Roger finished.

"Perhaps one item that could be on our company's cultural fit list would be that 'management candidates need to work as a team'. I mean, I want to see cooperation, support and respect for one another. None of that back-stabbing or finger-pointing I've seen in some other companies."

"That's a good one. You need managers who are team players," said Roger. "You have the right idea. A list of ten or so behavior patterns reflecting the cultural style of your company's best or most successful performers will be enough to compare to a candidate's past behavioral patterns."

I thought back about what Charles and Roger said. To ensure you hire the right person, know exactly what you expect the person to accomplish. Identify the specific results to be achieved during the first year, and use this list of performance expectations as part of the candidate evaluation process. This ties in with the premise that the best predictor of future performance is past performance.

Both Charles and Roger also stressed the need to hire someone whose cultural values and management style mesh with our management team. So it would make a lot of sense for us to put into writing the behavior patterns of our most successful people. Not a bad lesson for four holes.

11

Lesson One: Hire to Specific Performance Expectations

The process to hire extraordinary talent requires a recruitment definition based on specifically defined expectations for the person you are seeking. Many companies use job descriptions to define their hiring requirements. Unfortunately, job descriptions list duties and responsibilities, activities in which to indulge. A more useful approach to defining a hiring requirement begins with identifying the results you expect the new hire to achieve during the first year. The focus is on achieving results, or performance rather than just the duties or activities of a job.

Additionally, new hires need to fit in with your management style, and share your beliefs. This style is what is referred to as a company's culture, the values of which are typically set by the founders, owners or top management. Company culture needs to be identified, in writing, and based on the behavior patterns of your most successful employees. This list of behavior patterns should be a part of your recruitment definition.

Chapter Two

Implement a Proactive Recruitment Strategy

"Pat, let me introduce you to my second rule. I refer to it as '**Implement a Proactive Recruitment Strategy**'," he finished.

"Again using golf as an analogy, the USGA Rules of Golf say we can carry up to fourteen clubs in our bag. Roger, you and I usually carry the maximum; Harry often carries only eleven or twelve clubs because he usually walks the course and the load is lighter. With our handicaps, we need all the help we can get."

"A full set of tools for the job," I joked.

"Exactly my point. We have choices; we have a number of clubs from which to choose. Because we start a round of golf with a full set of clubs, we are prepared for what lies ahead of us."

"O.K. We are proactive in our thinking before we start playing," I said. "We don't wait until we are faced with a shot to determine if we had a particular club in our bag. We have all the clubs we need and hopefully are able to select the right club for any shot."

"Let's take that concept to your current hiring needs," Charles said. "You're looking for several high level executives, the sales vice president in particular, and you're starting the recruitment effort from scratch."

"Well, not exactly," I said somewhat defensively as I began to see where he was taking this.

"We have some resumes in our files, according to our HR Vice President, but we really don't know anything about them. I suppose we could have been more proactive and anticipated that we would have executive staffing needs in the future."

"Roger, you've put a good recruitment program in place in your company, share a few of your ideas with Pat," Charles stated.

"The most important thing we did to ensure a continuous flow of candidate prospects for our company was to hold each of our managers accountable for recruitment. We recognized early on that one of our most important assets, if not the most important, were our people. We needed to recruit and hire the best. That meant we always had to be looking for great additions to our staff—even when we didn't have an immediate need," Roger said.

"But what about your HR department, isn't that their job?" I asked.

"Pat, it certainly is an important part of their job. But it was the HR VP who prompted me to press all managers into being recruiters. After all, it's the total team that's makes the company successful," Roger responded. "We made every manager accountable for recruitment as part of his or her performance measurement, and consequently, as a part of their bonus consideration."

"If recruitment ties in with their compensation, I could see how managers would take that task seriously," I said. "What actions did your managers take to make it happen?"

"People at trade shows, conferences, and meetings, as well as other executives, like competitors, and customers, were all looked on as potential employees. Even social events became grounds for recruiting. One of our best marketing managers was found coaching our accounting manager's son's Little League team," Roger exclaimed.

"I find many of my sales people while walking the floors at trade shows," piped in Harry. "In fact, I steal them from competitors all the time. Trade shows are a great source to find many types of employees—from sales types to engineers. At one time or another, even the president of a company spends time on the trade show floor or greeting customers in his exhibit booth. It's easy to start up a conversation and get to know people. The trade show has been a great pool of talent from which to draw."

"Harry," said Charles, "Finding enough candidates and then selecting the ones that will be successful are two different issues. If you spent more time on selection, you wouldn't go through so many sales people."

"Our big industry trade show is in two weeks," I said. "There'll be hundreds of sales executive types. Great place to see them in action. This year I'll focus on meeting as many of them as I can, but with a specific purpose in mind; my new sales VP."

I've been to many trade shows over the past five years, but all of a sudden they became exciting. A treasure hunt. Thinking about the trade show possibility lifted my spirits.

"You should also consider bringing your key managers together and ask them to think about the people they've met over the past year—people who really attracted their attention and made a strong, positive impression on them. That should give you some names to begin your search," suggested Roger.

"Yeah, and tell your managers their bonuses depend on it," quipped Harry.

"If I want to keep my recruitment effort confidential, then I certainly can't ask the other managers for recommendations."

"The confidentiality part is something you need to address," responded Charles. "Personally, I would talk to the Sales VP and let him know that you plan to replace him, assuming you have had previous discussions with him regarding his lack of performance."

"I have had many talks with him, but he doesn't seem to get it," I said.

"A person who is not meeting performance expectations may know it, but not be able to face up to it or make the needed changes," said Charles. "The search process would be easier if he were told about being replaced. Then it would be all out in the open. However, if you decide to do the search confidentially, then you should consider an outside recruitment resource. Have you worked with any in the past?"

"You mean headhunters? At my last company we worked with one headhunter on several searches," I said. "She was quite successful in uncovering people we would not have found on our own. But I haven't spoken to her in two years."

Roger interrupted, "We developed a working relationship with one recruiter as part of our proactive recruitment strategy. We kept the recruiter tuned into our growth plans. In fact, we invited him to attend several of our management retreats and strategy sessions to gain a better understanding of our people and culture, and the direction we were taking our business. With this awareness, he alerted us to key people that he came across or knew. Over the years, most of our management team came through his efforts. This might be an approach you should consider.

"Another step our Human Resources VP took to ensure we had covered all the bases," Roger continued, "was to review the files of current employees and make a list of all their previous employers. Then, when a recruitment need suggested that a candidate come from certain targeted companies, she inquired of former colleagues and coworkers about the employee."

Our company needs to develop a proactive recruitment strategy that will ensure a continuous supply of candidates. We also need to get every manager involved in the recruitment process. To accomplish this, some sort of accountability has to be built into each manager's performance reviews.

This may all work well for future requirements, but I need to address our current hiring situation first. Roger suggested I get our team together to pull names of people they know. If I make this a priority issue, we may be able to speed up the process. I also need to address telling my Sales VP that he's history.

I'm much better off conducting this recruitment effort in the open. The pressure to fill this position immediately doesn't give me the luxury of keeping it confidential. Meanwhile, I need to identify an outside recruiter and begin to establish a working relationship with that person.

Lesson Two: Implement a Proactive Recruitment Strategy

People are your most important asset. Therefore you need to recruit and hire the best employees at all levels. To ensure a continuous flow of candidate prospects for your company means you always should be looking for great additions to your staff—even when you don't have an immediate need. Make every manager accountable for recruitment as part of his or her performance measurement, and consequently, as a part of their bonus consideration. Candidate sources are everywhere. People at trade shows, conferences, and meetings, as well as other executives, like competitors, and customers, should all be looked on as potential employees. Even social events become grounds for recruiting.

Develop a working relationship with a recruiter as part of your proactive recruitment strategy. Keep the recruiter tuned into your growth plans so that he or she can anticipate your needs.

With a proactive recruitment program in place, you don't start your candidate recruitment from scratch every time you have a need.

19

Chapter Three

Crack the Interview Façade

"Charles, what's the next rule?"

"I call it '**Crack the Interview Facade**'."

"The interview façade?"

"People usually put up a front when being interviewed. They want to make a good impression, so they embellish their accomplishments and play down their shortcomings. That's a natural reaction. They want to put their best foot forward. During the interview you need to get behind this façade and find out who the person really is," said Charles.

"I know what you mean. I've struggled through some interviews, knowing that the candidate is blowing smoke. I've tried a number of techniques to get at the real person. Sometimes they work, but sometimes it's frustrating. How do you know that you have really uncovered the person behind the mask?"

"You do it through interview probing techniques and then verify your findings through reference checking. But let's start with a few interview tips that might help you get to know the candidate better," Charles answered.

"Treat the interview as a narration of a person's life and accomplishments," said Charles. "I refer to it as a natural flow of information. I typically ask the candidate to trace his or her life from high school to the present, relating a chronology of events, work history and accomplishments."

"From high school?" I asked. "Are candidates really willing to go back that far?"

"If you make the request in a none-threatening manner, almost humorously, it plays very well. I often start by saying, 'I'm interested in understanding who you are and what you've accomplished. Why don't you begin with high school and tell your story from then to the present time.' By going from early career to current times, you can follow success patterns and relate them to your requirements," Charles said.

"Another axiom for good interviewing is to listen actively. Show interest in what the person is saying. Make short restatements or ask follow-up questions. They show your interest and invite further disclosure. Take notes. Do a lot of nodding to encourage more discussion. And ask for examples of what they have accomplished. I can't overstate the pursuit of examples. Probing the details of examples in which the candidate solved a problem or took some particular action provides insight into the candidate's thinking process.

"During some interviews I have asked candidates to solve problems," I stated. "It provides me an opportunity to see how they think on their feet. Although their answers may not be correct, I like to probe their assumptions and logic."

Charles smiled, and said," Problem solving is one of my favorite forms of getting behind the façade. If you keep probing, by asking the so-called editorials, like who, what, when, where, why and how, you'll have a much clearer picture of their past contributions and potential in your company."

"Pat," he said, "remember that past performance is the best predictor of future performance. So you want to make sure during the interview that you understand specifically what the candidate has personally accomplished, how he or she thinks, and get a feel for how the candidate's style would fit with your company's culture."

Roger interrupted, "Interviewing is a skill, and a skill that can be learned. Get in the habit of probing all candidate statements and you will get the most out of the interview. You didn't get so far in your career without developing some of these skills. It's a matter of organizing the interview in a logical fashion, like Charles said. His coaching helped our management stay on track."

Charles pointed his finger for emphasis. "One other important element of the interview is control. You ask the candidate to do the talking. Hold off telling the candidate what you are looking for or what your expectations are until the latter part of the interview."

"Yes," said Roger. "That was tough for me because I always wanted to brag about our company and the opportunities from the start of the interview."

"Roger hit the nail on the head," said Charles. "If you tell a candidate too much at the beginning of the interview, he or she will be able to feed back to you what they think you want to hear. It may not be an honest answer or comment, but may be biased toward your expectations. That's the façade we need to crack."

"Charles always talks about the 80/20 rule of interviewing," interrupted Roger. "If the candidate is talking eighty per cent of the time and you only speak twenty per cent of the time, then this usually results in a good interview."

"I've found that presidents, especially entrepreneurs, and sales people, (as he looks at Harry) are so enthusiastic and excited about their company and its products, that it's hard for them to keep quiet."

"Yeah, that's my problem in interviewing," said Harry. "I'm always selling something; the company, our products, the opportunity. I hardly give the candidate a chance to talk other than to verify what's on his resume."

"We made it a practice of having a candidate interviewed by a number of people in our company," Roger added. "This gives multiple readings on a candidate to ensure a proper fit."

"Did they all ask the same questions?" I asked.

"No, we divided up the task. For example, our HR department did a detailed review of the person's work history to make sure there are no missing gaps. Then the hiring manager concentrated on specific departmental contributions and cultural fit. Still others looked at how their particular activities would relate to the candidate. All in all, we felt that hiring was a very important process and we wanted to make darn sure we had the best candidate."

"Another word of caution," Charles jumped in. "Once you have read the resume or the candidate's application, put it away during the interview."

"I've used it as a guide for the interview," I said. "Is there something wrong with that?"

"Unfortunately," responded Charles, "having the resume in front of you may lead you to ask questions that are already answered on the resume, or questions that can be answered with a quick yes or no response. You become bound by the resume content.

Instead of using the resume during the interview, use it to prepare for the interview. Note red flags on the resume, like missing dates or positions that don't seem to indicate career progress. Ask about those red flags if they are not answered during the course of your chronological interview," he said.

"Keep in mind," added Roger, "the resume is a marketing tool, sometimes not even written by the candidate but by a professional resume service. Its only purpose is to get the candidate in the door for an interview. Treat it as a marketing tool, and remember to get behind the candidate façade."

I thought about the action I needed to take. I think my interviewing skills are pretty decent, but sometimes I do rely too much on the resume. I need to put it aside during the interview. I also have had a tendency to tell the candidate too much too soon, before we get into his discussion. I can see that in the past I have given the candidate too many clues, before the real interview began. I'm interviewing some very smart candidates, so I need to be on the alert to get behind the façade. Sort of like starting from a blank page and then trace the history from day one. It will be interesting to see the reaction of the candidate when I mention high school.

The key to a good interview is listening and probing.

Lesson Three: Crack the Interview Façade

People usually put up a front when being interviewed. Your job during the interview is to get behind this façade. To do this, treat the interview as a narration of a person's life and accomplishments. Start the interview from a candidate's early career and follow it to current times. Note candidate success patterns and relate them to your requirements as defined by performance expectations.

Interviewing is a skill which can be learned. Good interviewing starts with active listening. Show interest in what the candidate is saying. Take notes. Do a lot of nodding to encourage more discussion. Ask for examples. Problem solving is a good form of getting behind the façade. Keep probing, by asking the so-called editorials, like who, what, when, where, why and how. This will give you a much clearer picture of the candidate's past contribution and potential within your company.

One other important element of the interview is control. If you tell a candidate too much at the beginning of the interview, he or she will be able to feed back to you what they think you want to hear. It may not be an honest answer or comment, but may be biased toward

(continued)

your expectations. That's part of the façade you need to crack.

Past performance is the best predictor of future performance. Make sure you understand specifically what the candidate has personally accomplished, how he or she thinks, and how the candidate's style would fit with your company's culture.

Chapter Four

Don't Be Fooled by the Halo Effect

"OK, Charles, what's the fourth rule?"

"Let me start with an example," responded Charles. "Early on in Roger's company he had an outstanding salesperson. This woman could sell refrigerators to Eskimos. Turn her on to a prospect and you were almost guaranteed a sale. As the company grew, Roger wanted to reward Linda further by making her a regional sales manager. That turned out to be a big mistake."

"What happened? Promotions like that are done all the time. In fact we did the same a couple of years ago."

"I hope your experience was better than Roger's." Looking at Roger, I asked "So what happened to Linda?

With a grin he said,"Charles sure knows how to put a point across. Linda was good, that is, until I made some changes."

"What happened?"

"I assume Charles told you she was the best sales person we had at the time. As a reward for doing such a great job, I promoted her to a regional sales manager position. Unfortunately, I ended up with the worst of two worlds: we gained a rather weak regional sales manager and lost a stellar sales performer. I fell for the myth."

"What myth?" I asked.

"The myth that just because someone is top notch in one job, they automatically are going to be a top performer or very knowledgeable in another position. It's a false assumption that many people make. It's easy to be impressed with a person who is recognized for certain performance."

Charles jumped in: "That is the forth rule. I call it **'Don't be Fooled by the Halo Effect'**. It's a fairly common mistake made by hopeful, but perhaps undisciplined, hiring managers. They take for granted that a winning performance in one skill or situation is always transferable."

"I have seen other examples," added Roger. "When we were interviewing candidates to be a manager of one of our smaller, but growing divisions, we came across a general manager of a major division of one of the giant semiconductor companies. He had quite an impressive track record and was well known in the industry. We felt excited about the thought that he would even consider joining our company. However, after several very thorough interviews, thanks to Charles's coaching, we decided not to pursue him."

"What turned you off?" I asked.

"Although he appeared to be a solid candidate, probing indicated he was not the hands-on manager as we needed. He was aloof and distant from his team. He had created a management empire, which we would have difficulty accepting even in the best of times. In short, our lean-and-mean approach to running a business was not compatible with his style."

"The Halo Effect again," I said . . . "Assuming one will be good in areas other than where they have been recognized as a hero, so to speak."

"That's just like in golf," added Harry. "You don't see the top winners from the Long-Drive contests on the PGA Tour. They've mastered the long drive, but that specialty doesn't carry over to the rest of their game."

"You see this in product promotion all the time on TV," commented Charles. "Celebrity spokespersons endorsing a product, not necessarily because they use it, but because they are paid to say they use it. This gives the viewing consumer the impression that the celebrity likes the product. Just note some of the product endorsements on The Golf Channel info-commercials and you will see how easy it is to fall for the Halo Effect."

"It's not difficult to overcome the Halo Effect. You need to be disciplined in your selection process."

"What do you mean?"

"Two of the steps in the hiring process will void the Halo Effect; good probing during the interview and probing equally as hard when checking references. By probing, I mean digging for examples of what the person has accomplished, their management style, and how they work with others. Don't treat what they say as gospel, but continue to probe until you feel comfortable you've gotten behind the façade."

That "Halo Effect" seems pretty easy to avoid. It boils down to making sure the reason for a candidate's high level of performance is transferable to our performance expectations.

Lesson Four: Don't be Fooled by the Halo Effect

Superstar performance may not apply to your situation. That happens when you assume outstanding performance by a candidate in one particular facet of his or her job will apply to the performance you expect of a candidate in a different position. Skills and experience are not always transferable from one position to another or from one company culture to another. For example, the skills that have made a person very successful in selling a product or service are quite different than the skills required to be a sales manager. Or, a candidate who has been a leader in a large corporation may not have the attributes to lead a small entrepreneurial organization.

Two steps in the hiring process will void the Halo Effect. First, during the interview, probe the candidate for examples of his or her performance and style to compare to your requirements. And second, when speaking with candidate references, probe equally as hard for specific examples of performance. Describe the performance you expect of the individual you are hiring, and ask the reference person for examples of similar performance.

The "Halo Effect" may be awe striking, but don't let it over shadow your requirements.

Chapter Five

Don't Shortcut the Hiring Process

"O.K., what's the fifth rule?" I asked.
"It's **'Don't Shortcut the Hiring Process'**,"
Charles replied. "That's just wishful thinking."

"Taking shortcuts or wishful thinking often happens when you're just trying to fill a position as opposed to hiring someone to meet specific performance expectations."

"What do you mean?"

"When you have specific results or performance expectations in mind, you're looking for examples of like performance during the interview. In a sense, it forces you to probe deeper to ensure the candidate could really meet your expectations.

"If you just look for someone to fill a position without considering targeted performance for them, it is less likely you will probe as deep. Wishful thinking usually ends up in breaking the rules and ignoring or skipping part of the hiring process needed to hire for results. In other words, you end up shortcutting the entire hiring process"

In thinking about what Charles just said, I can recall when I hired the current Vice President of Sales, the one I am now replacing. I needed someone quickly to manage the sales force. I hadn't gone through the development of a list of performance expectations. In some respects, I lost sight of what I wanted to accomplish. I just wanted to fill the vacant position, and hire someone like the previous incumbent, only better. The problem was, I didn't know what "better" meant.

I've learned my "wishful thinking" lesson the hard way. The Vice President of Sales fiasco proved the point. He was a successful regional sales person in a much larger, well known company. His former company's brand and reputation made it easy for him to get his foot in the customer's door. Our company is still establishing its position and name. Without a large, established firm and name behind him, his skills were not transferable. He didn't know how to make it happen. I must concentrate on following all the hiring steps to ensure I hire someone who will meet our performance expectations.

Lesson Five: Don't Shortcut the Hiring Process

When you have a hiring requirement, the path of least resistance is to find someone like the person who previously occupied that position. However, business is dynamic, and so are the requirements of individuals to be successful. Performance goals change. Thus, looking for someone to fill a position without considering targeted performance can result in hiring the wrong candidate.

Not going through the process of defining performance expectations or goals leads to a process that can best be identified as "Wishful Thinking." Wishful thinking becomes the "hope" for making the hire. Wishful thinking usually ends up in breaking the rules and ignoring or skipping part of the hiring process needed to hire for results.

A thorough hiring process reduces the inherent risk in making a hire. It helps a hiring manager make a more objective and predictable hiring decision.

Chapter Six

Make Intuition Work for You

"O.K., what's this sixth rule?"

"**'Make Intuition Work for You'**," he said.

"Think about the hiring decision-making process. You have interviewed a candidate, and all the responses seem to be right on. But there is something in your gut that bothers you about the candidate. Could be as complicated as a lack of trust in what the candidate said. Or it could be as simple as thinking this person will not be fun to work with. In either case something bothers you about this candidate that you really can't quite put your finger on.

"Intuition can play an important part in your hiring decision. It's based on a feeling from some event or situation in the past that triggers a notion about the candidate. This notion can be a positive one or a negative one. Intuitive feelings can point to an area that needs further exploration. Don't ignore intuition. As I have said many times, when in doubt, check it out."

"I got good at this intuitive thing," Roger said to us all, but specifically looking at me. "After you've interviewed as many people as I have, you get this feeling in your gut that a person is either a strong contender for the position or should be dropped as a candidate.

"As Charles has often said, when in doubt, don't hire the person until you have checked out this doubt. There is always some risk in hiring even if you did everything correctly. When there is this gut feeling, check it out with references."

I recalled an incident that reminded me of this last sin. After my wife and I had dinner with a candidate from Texas, my wife said she thought they would never move to Sacramento. I asked her why, and she said it was just a feeling she had after listening to the conversation. The candidate accepted our offer and moved to Sacramento. My wife was wrong, that is, until six months later when they moved back to Texas. That demonstrated my need to listen to gut feelings, or at least my wife's intuition.

Lesson Six: Make Intuition Work for You

Intuition can play an important part in your hiring decision. Don't ignore intuitive feelings. They are generally based on your reaction from some event or situation in the past that triggers a notion about the candidate. Something in your gut bothers you about the candidate. It could be as complicated as a lack of trust in what the candidate said, or it could be as simple as thinking this person will not be fun to work with.

Intuitive feelings can be positive or negative. They point to areas that need further exploration. Use this intuitive signal to probe further during the interview and with individuals you speak when checking employment references. When in doubt, check it out.

Chapter Seven

Check One More Reference

Roger looked at me and said, "Remember what Charles said about references verifying your gut feel. Well, I think reference checking is the most important step you can take to ensure what you see is what you get. References reduce the risk in making a hiring decision."

Charles commented, "Roger just introduced the seventh rule, '**Check One More Reference**'."

"What do you mean by 'one more reference'? How do you know when you've reached that last reference?"

"You'll know that when you receive consistent reports from the people you speak with about the candidate. Not just the names that the candidate gave you to contact, but additional people who you uncover in the process," Charles responded.

"Who I uncover?"

"Yes. One question you must ask every reference you speak with is, 'Who else should I talk to who could provide me with more insight into the candidate's capabilities?' I always assume that individuals given to me as references by the candidate were prompted in advance of my call. Although that may not always be the case, you expand your knowledge and reduce your hiring risk by speaking with others about the candidate."

"I guess that's what it's all about," I said, "reducing hiring risks."

"The whole reference checking process is based on the principle that past performance is the best predictor of future performance. After interviewing a candidate, you draw certain tentative conclusions about the candidate. Strengths, shortcomings, work behavior style, and concerns that need clarification or amplification. References should verify your conclusions, answer any concerns or stimulate further questions to ask the candidate in a follow-up interview."

"Reference checking is so important that in my company I insisted that every person hired must have had at least four references checked," said Roger. "In fact, anyone who was being hired for a professional or management position had to have at least two references checked that were not names given by the candidate."

"I recall one situation where a company was hiring a General Manager," said Charles, "and references beyond the ones provided by the candidate were quite revealing. One reference person contacted, who was a customer, said the candidate had exhibited inappropriate behavior toward her. Another customer painted a similar picture. The candidate, who was qualified technically and had good initial references, was immediately dropped from consideration."

Even Harry got into the act. "I checked the references on a super regional sales manager candidate who had accepted our offer of employment pending our reference checking."

"Not a good practice," interrupted Charles. "That can get you into trouble."

"Yeah, I know," continued Harry. "This guy was on his first day on the job when I started my reference calls. Boy, what a mistake we had made! He had lied about receiving a degree and had more jobs than those listed on his resume and discussed during the interview. Fortunately these were factual items that we could confront him with. We walked him out the door, checked him out of his hotel and dropped him at the airport. He had the nerve to send us an expense invoice for three more days in our city. He actually went back to the hotel for several days and thought we would pay for it."

"References, the backbone for a go no-go decision," I mumbled.

"The most reliable reference information you can get is from your friends, colleagues or former employees," Charles continued. "That is one strong reason to maintain your network of contacts. You usually can reach someone who knows someone who knows the candidate or people who have worked with the candidate. Not only should these references be most revealing, but they may also provide you with recommendations of additional candidates for the position. I've seen more than one reference call turn into a candidate referral."

"We have tried to obtain reference information from Human Resources people," I said, "but all we get are the standard dates of employment and title. Useful, but not insightful."

"Human Resources personnel are protecting their company from the possibility of a libel suit," said Charles. "That's their responsibility. But they usually are not much help when you are trying to discover candidate capabilities and behavioral patterns."

"Probing is the key to obtaining revealing reference information," added Roger. "Use the same techniques you would employ during the interview. Ask for examples and push for details."

Charles said, "I would add that whenever you can meet with a reference individual in person, do so. You're bound to learn more about the candidate just from observing and listening for nuances and voice inflections. It is also harder for people to hold back answering questions when being interviewed face-to-face."

Still concerned about references, I asked, "What approach do you suggest to check references on someone who has worked for one company for the past ten years, and is still employed by that company?"

"Let me try to answer that one," Roger said. "Let's assume that everything has gone well during the interviews and you and the candidate would like to proceed. You should indicate very clearly to the candidate that references are required before any offer could be extended. The candidate tells you he or she needs to keep the prospect of leaving the present employer confidential or else the employer may get upset and even find an excuse to fire the person."

"O.K., so what can you do," I asked.

"Ask the candidate for names of people who have recently left the company or people within the company who know about the candidate's interest in making a change of employment," responded

Roger. "Most people who are looking tend to tell someone. The important point to get across to the candidate is that references are a must to continue employment discussions."

I thought about the last sin. Several recent hires came to mind. Did I push for enough reference information? Have I've been too accepting of candidates as they presented themselves. Have I been too much a "Mr. Nice Guy?" The bottom line is that I need to find out as much as I can about a candidate before making an employment offer.

Lesson Seven: Check One More Reference

Reference checking is a way of ensuring that what you see in the candidate is what you are going to get. After interviewing a candidate, you draw certain tentative conclusions about the candidate. Strengths, shortcomings, work behavior style and other concerns that need clarification or amplification. References should verify your conclusions, answer any concerns or stimulate further questions to ask the candidate in a follow-up interview.

Reference contacts need to go beyond just the people the candidate gave you to contact. Although you use interviewing probing techniques, you should assume that the names given by the candidate have been "primed" to give you a glowing report. Consequentially, additional reference names need to be contacted; names that you discover during the reference checking process. Ask each reference person you speak with for additional people who could provide more insight into the candidate's capabilities. The whole reference checking process is based on the principle that past performance is the best predictor of future performance.

Chapter Eight

Afterwards

It was getting close to 9:00 o'clock. I looked at
Charles, and said, "Thanks for helping me this
morning. I really do appreciate your advice." Then
addressing Roger, "Your experiences were very
helpful. We need to talk some more." And finally
looking over at Harry, "Harry, what can I say.
Maybe it was a lesson for the both of us."

Too all, "I'm under a lot of pressure right now.
I knew you would have some thoughts and ideas to
help with this problem. And I was right. Those
seven rules certainly spoke to some of my hiring
blunders. Now I need to make a list of action items
to implement these rules."

"Judging by your pressing hiring need for a
sales vice president, you better get that action plan
going fast," said Charles. "I'll email you the outline
I used for my presentation of the Seven Rules when
I get back to the office, if that will help. Then you
can start working on your action items over the
weekend."

"Thanks, Charles," I responded. "Do you have
some time this coming week to meet with my management group to provide a basis for the action
items?"

"You're in luck, my friend," Charles said. "My
monthly coaching session with a long-time client
next Tuesday got cancelled. They have an important

customer opportunity that will take most of their management team to San Diego that day."

"Pat, I'm glad you're getting Charles involved this time," added Roger. "His coaching and guidance helped us hire some great people."

When we left The Perfect Blend, Charles reassured me that the email would be sent by evening. We decided to meet at my office at ten on Tuesday morning for a two-hour discussion with my management group. We are going to concentrate on our hiring process and interview techniques.

I was really pumped, and anxious to get things rolling. I even thought of calling my Human Resources VP on my cell phone, to share some of the ideas, but that could wait until I got to the office.

* * *

Friday morning. Seven a.m. Charles had emailed his outline last evening, as promised. I wanted to review it with my HR VP so she would have a "heads up" on the plan for Charles on Tuesday. Responding to my earlier email, she arrived at my office just before eight.

I filled her in on the events that took place on Thursday and then went over Charles' notes that I had printed out.

Seven Rules for Hiring Extraordinary Talent

1. Hire to Specific Performance Expectations
   a) Forget job descriptions
   b) Develop measurable performance expectations
   c) Identify behavior patterns for successful cultural fit

2. Implement a Proactive Recruitment Strategy
   a) Management accountability for sourcing candidates
   b) Partner with an outside recruitment person

3. Crack the Interview Façade
   a) Interview style—natural flow of information
   b) Active listening—without resume
   c) Problem solving and examples
   d) Control! Don't sell before you discover

4. Don't Be Fooled by the Halo Effect
   a) Assuming a carry-over of talent
   b) Verify through interview and references

5. Don't Shortcut the Hiring Process
   a) Taking shortcuts—skipping process

(continued)

6. Make Intuition Work for You
   a) Pay attention to gut feelings
   b) When in doubt, check it out

7. Check one More Reference
   a) Gain consensus of opinion
   b) Ask interview-like questions
   c) Go beyond response from HR

As we reviewed Charles' outline, it became crystal clear. We don't hire people just to fill a position. Rather, we hire an employee to meet or exceed performance expectations. If past performance is the best predictor of future performance, then knowing the future performance we desire is mandatory for a good hiring program.

The seven rules Charles described in his speech were really practices one needs to follow in order to hire extraordinary talent. And it all begins with developing a list of performance expectations- the results we expect this person to achieve. All the other hiring steps—recruiting, interviewing and reference checking—are steps to identify, compare and verify the candidate's past performance with what we expect in future performance.

With my HR VP, we began to develop a hiring campaign, which would be kicked off with the management meeting tomorrow with Charles. We began a list of action items:

1. All hiring requirements will begin with a list of performance expectations created by the hiring manager. Either the HR VP or I will need to sign-off on these performance expectations to initiate the hiring process. This will include recruitment efforts for both replacement position as well as new positions.

2. We will hold a management meeting to identify the behavior patterns that are typical of our most successful employees. These behavior patterns will reflect our company's core values, and the culture we have created.

3. Managers will be held accountable for identifying and bringing to our attention outstanding people they have met in all walks of life. Business related conferences and meetings, social gatherings, and even just reading or hearing about someone who could help our company grow, will be catalogued by the HR department. Part of a manager's performance expectations will be this proactive recruitment effort. This performance will tie into their compensation plan.

4. We will hire Charles to conduct a workshop on how to develop performance expectations and how to interview candidates to determine they meet these expectations. Our HR VP will develop follow-up training and coaching.

5. Reference checking will be mandatory, no matter how well we think we know the candidate. Reference information will be

obtained from at least two people whose names were not supplied by the candidate. Reference checking should be as probing as interview questions.

6. We will form an alliance with a recruiter to help us get a head start on important recruitment needs. As part of the alliance, the recruiter will be invited to attend our management strategy sessions for a better understanding of future recruitment needs.

The above list of action items will be a good start. Our mission on Tuesday is to get full buy-in from the rest of the management team. I know between Charles, our HR VP and I, we'll make it happen.

* * *

Tuesday noon. Charles led a discussion on the seven rules and encouraged a results driven hiring attitude with our management. Prior to breaking for lunch I addressed the management group. "Employees are our most important asset. If we can attract and hire the best people, then we greatly improve our opportunities for success. To accomplish this, we need to implement this results-driven hiring practice throughout the organization. In the beginning it may take a little more work for all of us, but the rewards will be there. Now, let's make it happen!"

* * *

One month later. Our foursome met at the
Granite Bay Golf Club, where Charles was a
member.

"Well, how is your Sales VP recruitment effort
coming?" asked Roger. Roger and I had lunch with
my HR VP, just after Charles made his two-hour
presentation. Roger was quite helpful in suggesting
a few thoughts on additional training. "When we
had lunch, you and your HR VP were all fired up
about your results-driven hiring campaign."

"Yeah, Pat, do tell before we get to the first tee,"
joked Harry. "Let's not make this a scholarly day."

"The first thing I did was to develop a list of
performance expectations for the Sales VP position.
That was our most important recruitment need at the
time. Doing that exercise before going to the trade
show really helped. Concentrating on the results I
expected the Sales VP to achieve, I uncovered several people who had some of those same experiences. Discussions were much more focused.

"Did you speak with your current Sales VP,
you know, about his performance?" asked Roger.

"I told him we were going to replace him."

"How did that discussion go?" asked Roger.
"You were going to do it after our lunch that day."

"At first he acted surprised. Then I showed him
the list of performance expectations I had created.
Although we had not had that list formally when he
was hired, we had discussed specific goals a number of times. The more we talked he faced up to his
lack of performance, and seemed to feel relieved.
Especially, when I told him we would keep him on
until his replacement was found.

"Meanwhile, we would consider him for other positions within the company, provided we thought he would be successful in meeting those performance expectations. If not, we were prepared to give him one month of severance pay."

"Performance expectations are very useful in evaluating internal candidates for other positions," interjected Charles. "In fact, every position in a company should have performance expectations. In that way the objectives of the position are clear to both the incumbent and his or her supervisor. Just a side benefit of a results driven hiring program."

"Charles is scheduled to conduct his full-day hiring workshop with our management next week," I said, looking over at Charles. "This will reinforce the skills needed to interview and evaluate candidates as they are uncovered."

"Our HR VP spoke with each member of the executive team to see if they knew of someone who could be a candidate for the Sales VP position. Several names were mentioned. We have been contacting those individuals to determine their interest."

"Have you hooked up with a recruiter?" asked Charles.

"We're interviewing two of them next week. Even developed performance expectations for our relationship with the recruiter," I added proudly.

"What about that cultural thing we discussed last month?" asked Harry. I thought he wasn't paying any attention to our discussion, so his question took me by surprise.

"Harry, as Roger did with his management, we are planning on doing that during Charles' workshop next week. Right Charles?"

"We could spend about an hour on that," said Charles. "It's important to know what behavior patterns work best in your company. And it's important that your management team shares and agrees on these behavior patterns."

There wasn't any more discussion as we approached the first tee. I think everyone had enough of this for the time being. I'm excited about putting in place this results-driven hiring process that will help us hire extraordinary talent.

About the Author

Richard J. Pinsker, CMC, FIMC is President of
Pinsker and Company, an executive selection
consulting firm. He coaches executives on how to
hire people who exceed expectations, and conducts
retained search engagements for board members,
presidents and CEOs, and the full executive team.

Mr. Pinsker has helped thousands of hiring
managers make more objective and predictable
employee selection decisions. He conducts
corporate workshops based on the P.I.E. Selection
System, introduced in his first book, *Hiring
Winners*, now in its seventh printing. A recognized
professional speaker, he has presented to trade and
professional associations and has appeared on
nationally syndicated talk shows. His numerous
articles on executive selection have been published
throughout the world.

He is a Certified Management Consultant, an
elected Fellow of the Institute of Management
Consultants, and holds degrees in psychology from
the University of Wisconsin. He resides in Granite
Bay, California and can be reached at:
916–797–9166 or richard@pinskerandco.com.

Advance Praise from Business Leaders

"Pinsker has unveiled the key secrets of the value of hiring good managers and made his important tools available in a very novel style of presentation that is both educational and entertaining. I recommend his book to everyone who wants to gain control of their hiring practices for good managers . . ."

– Robert Wolfe, former Chairman, GenCorp.

" . . . I found the story line easy to read and follow . . . significantly helps making better hiring decisions."

– Robert Lorber, PhD., Co-Author,
Putting the One Minute Manager to Work

"This is a thoroughly enjoyable book, yet loaded with valuable principles and insight. Anyone involved in the hiring process will benefit from the methods presented, which address the common hiring mistakes."

– Peter F .Bernardoni, Managing Director,
Wavepoint Ventures

"If hiring top level employees is your goal, then *Seven Rules for Hiring Extraordinary Talent* is must reading. It's an easy, fast, fun read while learning how to avoid the most common hiring mistakes."

– John Hounslow, Chairman/Founder,
Mt. Diablo Bank

58

"How I wish I had this book years ago when I struggled to build a staff for my business. It would have saved me several hiring mistakes. Pinsker's *Seven Rules for Hiring Extraordinary Talent* is right on."

– E Michael Shays, CMC, FIMC,
Author of *Focused or Failed Leadership*